TOMBSTONES

TOMBSTONES

SELECTED HORROR POEMS
BY G. O. CLARK

Trade Paperback Edition

No part of this publication may be reproduced, stored or transmitted in any form or by any means, electronic, mechanical, photocopying, recording, scanning, or otherwise without written permission from the publisher. It is illegal to copy this book, post it to a website, or distribute it by any other means without permission.

ISBN: 978-1-957121-31-4

Text © 2001 - 2022 by G. O. Clark

Interior and cover design by Cyrusfiction Productions

Editor and Publisher, Joe Morey

Weird House Press
Central Point, OR 97502

www.weirdhousepress.com

Dedicated to Ian, Kim, and Lilly.

Table of Contents

Selected Poems (2001–2008)

Again the Night Too Deep	2
How to Detect a Ghost	4
His Lady in Red	5
Vicodins And Voodoo Dolls	6
One Last Dance Before The Oblivion Express	7
Mary Has A Prophetic Vision	8
Lady Robotica	9
Midnight Dread	10
Sensory Overload	11
Teeth	12
Grin	13
The End	14
The Desert Of Time	15
Five Statements	16

Selected Poems (2009-2013)

Mortician's Tea	18
Halfway Home	19
9 Dark Cinquains	20
Extinction	22
Hunter and Prey	23
Our Town	24
A Bloody Baker's Dozen	26
Restaurant Tale	29

Lamp	30
Uninvited Guest	31
Fear	33
The Stranger	34
Only On Dying Lips	35
Sailing with the Devil	36
This Part of Town	38
The Head	39
Ghosts Of Dead Children	40
Seasons of the Living Dead	41
Zombie Clowns	42
Zombie On A Leash	43
Zombie Loner	44
Writer's Block	45
Albino	46
Rag Doll	47
Reanimated	48
Two Drink Minimum	50
Scarecrow	51
Some Zombies One Should Avoid	52
The Last Zombie	54

Selected Poems (2014-2018)

The Party Crashers Scenario	56
The Darkness Within	57
The White Sedan	58
Dark Forest	60
A Stone Angel's Tears	61
Head Games	62

The Taste of Death	63
If Only the Leaves Could Talk	64
The Lost Maiden's Secrets	65
Ghost Coda	66
The Waiting Shadows	68
Preserves	69
The Sea Monster	70
Gravediggers' Dance	71
Endgame	72
Parting Shots	73
Redeye	74
The Comfort Of Screams	76
Postcard From The Night Desert	77
Nesting Habits Of The Mutant Crows	78
Her Apparition Walked Right Through Him	79
Scents Upon A Delta Breeze	80
A Tale Of Blood & Gasoline	82
Dark Angels Descending	84
Cthulhu's Checklist	85
The Mortician's Daughter	86
Rock On	87
Hitchhiker	88
Corn Maze	89
The Coroner	90
Postmortem Regret	92
Cataclysm	93
At The Spa	94
The Unraveling	95

New Poems (2019-2022)

Leisureville	98
Caged Fear	99
Weeds	101
A Darker Shade Than Normal	103
A Very Limited Engagement	104
Hoping For A Menu Change	105
A Hole In The Dark	106
Of Wood Chippers & Band Saws	107
A Smell Of Coffee And Sulfur	109
Leaving The Past Behind	110
Oblivion's Realm	112
Dead Men Walking	114
A Crime Of Passion	115
Ghosts Of Christmas Past	116
Tiny Houses Of The Forgotten	118
The Arms Of Death	119
Selfies	120
Demon Weather	121
The Darkness Behind The Dark	123
Acknowledgement	124
Publication History: Books, Chapbooks,& Magazines	125
About the Author	126

R.I.P.

Selected Poems 2001-2008

Again the Night Too Deep

One should never
be left alone in a vacuum,
a speck in space and time.

Objects appear where
nothing was before, spectral
planets so like home.

You hear the sound
of rain pitter-pattering upon
the outside hull,

but the view ports
don't back up your ears, the
stars dryly shining.

The warm smell
of fresh bread baking replaces
that of stale oxygen,

metal walls softening,
an olfactory illusion in this freeze
dried, squeeze-tube world.

You dream of her touch
once again, hands massaging your
tired neck muscles,

arms encircling your
chest, whisper-breath in ear, silken hair
against your stubbly cheek.

There's a metal aftertaste
in your mouth, perhaps from blood
or gunpowder,

that could be real, or just
the special effects of the dream works,
the scenario never played out.

In the darkened command
center, the ghost of someone reflected
in the front view port,

bone white hair, blackened
eye sockets, a permanent sneer at the
corner of its cracked, dead lips.

How to Detect a Ghost

The politically correct ones
usually wear tee shirts with the words
Existence Impaired printed in bold letters
across the front.

After arriving home each day,
to your swinging bachelor pad, you find
the television turned on and tuned
to the History Channel.

Each morning you find lengthy,
silent messages left on your answering
machine, and you're pretty sure
they're not meant for you.

Things keep disappearing,
then suddenly reappearing, but
hard as you try, you can't seem to keep
track of which ones are which.

Your cat, who used to sleep
at the foot of your bed, now sleeps in
the garage curled up on the hood
of the Volvo; her bags packed.

His Lady in Red

The woman
in the red cape drifts
by his window,

cold winter day
wrapped around her like
and icy aura,

her spectral
presence visible only to
his painter's eye,

their amorous past
his to apply to the purity
of the canvas;

that white field
of physicality where paint
and brush embrace,

and two spirits
become as one again in
time and space.

Vicodins And Voodoo Dolls

You have a voodoo doll that looks like me.
I always keep a morphine drip ready at hand.

You cast dream spells my way at midnight.
I stay awake all night watching late-night TV.

You leave anonymous curses on my answering machine.
I have caller ID, and erase them without listening.

You plant poisonous spiders between my sheets.
I fling them to the floor where my cat patiently waits.

You once went so far as to hire a crack assassin.
I offered him more to reverse the favor, but he failed.

We both have one thing in common, however.
The complete inability to finish whatever we start.

I have a voodoo doll that looks like you.
You pop pain killers like candy, and sleep like a baby.

One Last Dance Before
The Oblivion Express

She comes smelling of old perfume, dirt and
rotting flesh, her long white hair a tangle of twigs and
spider webs falling limply down her bent back.

The faded black gown she wears is moth eaten
and clings to her skeletal frame, like an old muslin sheet
draped over the bones of some ancient mummy.

Her callused feet are bare, toenails green and
horn-like, and her face, her face juts out like the crucified
figurehead upon the prow of Satan's frigate,

weathered by an eternity upon the burning sea,
shrunken into a horrible caricature of its once proud self.
Her cracked lips form a toothless hooker's smile,

and her black eyes are crystallized orbs: holocaust
snap shots, genocidal flashbacks, and memories of her
lifetime tour through the heart of man trapped within.

She comes, her ring adorned claws stretching towards
you, your soul to glide around the killing floor, foul nothings
whispered in your ear; dance card not yet full.

Another cricket to appease the Beast, our band leader
for the evening, waving his fiery baton to the maddening beat,
Oblivion Express panting just outside the fire door.

Mary Has A Prophetic Vision

She provides the good doctor
with the skeleton of a dress form,
the eyes of a ventriloquist's dummy,
the pointy ears of Nick Bottom,
and the voice of a drunken Greek god,
and he in turn sews them all together
beneath a California tan.

Yet her creation is still incomplete,
so she borrows the heart from the Tin Man,
the right brain from his friend the Scarecrow,
and the balls from their buddy the Cowardly Lion.
Then with the innards of an old fashioned clock,
a little juice and a prayer, instructs the
good doctor to finish the job.

Their monster fully alive at last,
she sends him forth to face fire and ice,
love and hate, bondage and freedom,
bad haircuts and sloppy tailors,
all within the time frame of a melting clock,
through a landscape full of stairways leading
nowhere, and good-citizen torch bearers
out to set the night on fire.

Finally, her vision about to fade,
she observes the last chapter of her little tale,
the monster abandoned on the ice and left to die,
the good doctor defrocked and sent into exile,
the dull villages returning to their dull routines,
and the author long dead before Hollywood
dividends could come her way.

Lady Robotica

She comes for you,
pale red lips, mahogany eyes,
and tightly curled copper wire
hair cascading down her bare,
metallic shoulders.

Your bones are but
balsa wood in her embrace,
and your flesh a practice hide
for this tattoo artist's painfully
intimate caress.

She sings as she works,
a deadly siren voice building
to an electronic harpy chorus;
a victory song celebrating the
extinction of your kind.

When it's finally over,
she tosses you aside like a
picked clean side of beef, stiletto
heels kicking up sparks; new lover
already in the cross hairs.

G. O. Clark

Midnight Dread

The rain has let up but for
a bit of Chinese water torture,
the liquid mercury droplets
plunking upon my roof.

Beneath the cloud
enshrouded moon, an owl
solemnly lifts from his perch,
the hunt no longer delayed.

My cat sits at the foot
of the bed, ears attuned to the
rain droplets and hooting owl,
roughly cleaning her paws.

There's something out
there this night, not fully formed,
the misty outline of pure darkness
stalking the unwary.

When the scream finally
comes, it's almost a relief, the beast
sated, some other soul sacrificed;
my covers now eased back.

Sensory Overload

Out of the alley's
shadows, the black
shape of the one you fear,
discerned too late to
make your escape.

Its dark embrace
enshrouds you, those
trademark canines planting
a jagged kiss upon your
warm, pulsing jugular.

A combined smell
of cigarette smoke, moth balls,
animal musk, foul gutter water
and fresh blood permeate
your final breath.

Your lifeblood is
the last thing you taste,
a final drop placed upon your
dry, parted lips by its
bone cold finger.

The guttural sound
of its feasting, church bells
chiming in the distance, and your
own stifled scream are the
last sounds you hear.

Teeth

His teeth
were first to go
not the ever sharp canines
the other ones that helped form
a dark leer.

Grin

She made
a fetish from
the dried skin of his soul
fashioned a death mask complete with
his grin.

The End

Clever
little cockroach
outlived him in the end
danced on his grave just for the
fun of it.

The Desert Of Time

Deep within the boundaries
of the desert of time

lay dark secrets long past
their statute of limitations,

unmarked graves
of good intentions never filled,

articles of faith abandoned
after too many years of hoping,

the rusting wrecks of desperate
measures too late in coming,

a bullet riddled sign marking
the waters of remembrance,

scorched pieces of the alien
puzzle littering the sunbaked past,

and ghost towns along the human
timeline, abandoned by the mind.

G. O. Clark

Five Statements

The ballerinas
have all turned to stone,
their music frozen in mid-note,
the stage a checkerboard of land minds.

Look closely,
each tear falling from the young girl's eyes
holds the reflection of another face
shrouded by war.

The square is cluttered
with the larger than life statues of tyrants,
just enough room between each one
for the rats to run freely.

The madwoman raises
her birdhouses on hundred foot poles,
high above the treading combat boots,
high into the sun cleansed sky.

Coming from the fog
the hollow drone of TV network news,
and distant fog horns warning
all those upon the black hearted sea.

Mortician's Tea

The mortician
works at his trade
consoling those left behind,
selling fresh coffins
like an unobtrusive car salesman,
respecting the wishes
of the recently deceased
to join with the waiting worms,
or be sealed against time
in shiny metal urns,

his life
one of quiet reverence
and solemn tradition,
his only deviation
from professional routine,
a spoonful of ashes
stirred into the afternoon tea.

Halfway Home

The madwoman
spends her days debating
with scarecrows,

harping
free verse to the marble
cemetery angels,

and sitting on
park benches, surrounded
by attentive ghosts.

At night she
laughs at TV sitcoms only
she can see and hear,

shares snacks of
milk and cookies with the
milk carton children,

and gets tucked in by
the gentle hands of a giant,
attuned to her delusions.

9 Dark Cinquains

The skull
on the bookshelf
a trophy of a sorts
won the hard way in the hot pits
of Hell.

❦

Mangled
in a train wreck
wired back together
kids call him old man smelly guts
and run.

❦

Old hag
pull-my-string doll
croaks out obscenities
a different one for each child
she knew.

❦

His head
nicely shrunken
hangs on rearview mirror
of the black Cadillac he once
gave her.

❦

The eyes
had a way of
staring right back at him
long after being pried from their
sockets

❈

Bus load
of cadavers
en route to casino
unaware their chips already
cashed in.

❈

Herr Doktor
comes a calling
replaces her aching heart
with another dark as the well
of night.

❈

Shallow
graves are the best
less trouble for the dead
when the time's ripe to scare the
living.

❈

Back yard
on moonless night
hides every kind of fear
remembered by the old and weak
of heart.

Extinction

The reflection of
the archer in the last
dragon's eyes.

King Kong's
swan dive onto 5th Ave.
far below.

Frankenstein
kneeling upon the ice flow,
breath crystallizing.

T-Rex's curious
gaze as the fireball falls
from the sky

The fear in the
ape man's eyes as the femur
cracks his skull.

Hunter and Prey

It's the sounds
the old one makes
that freezes you in
your tracks.

That arthritic
crackling of bones,
whip-like snapping of
tendons and muscle,

the grinding of
its jagged, bloody
teeth, and that deep,
nasal wheezing,

each wet breath
accompanying another
heavy footfall bearing
down upon you,

footfalls forgotten
when that chalk-on-
blackboard screech
issues from the

dark hole of
its mouth, echoing in
the darkness, ripping
your mind in two.

It's the sound
the old one makes,
the hunter devouring
its fallen prey.

G. O. Clark

Our Town

There's a family of cannibals
living across the street. If you didn't
know better, you'd swear they had the
same appetites as the rest of us.

Down the dark alleys of the old
warehouse district, zombies are said
to lurk, posing as old winos, or
half-way house rejects.

Mechanical hearts beat
beneath the blue uniforms and
shiny badges of our esteemed police,
the latest from T-Robotics,
if the truth be told.

The butchers behind the counter
at Corelli's are rumored to like warm
blood; vampires of a sort, connoisseurs
of the rarest of rare meats.

Of course our mayor is a shape shifter.
The doctors practice voodoo medicine.
Father Francis caters to Satan.
And the children here all have *some* power.

Our town is not unlike other towns.
Civic pride and community spirit are always
alive and well here. The annual harvest
celebrations attended by all.

This year's solstice bonfire
will burn brighter than ones past;
the lost casino bus, with a blown engine,
proving to be a real Godsend.

A Bloody Baker's Dozen

One is for
sweet Sarah Anne, alone
now in her grave, put there by her
boyfriend Ned, quite an expert
with a stave.

Two is for
the Remington babies,
missing fifty years, their mother
growing senile, running low
on crocodile tears.

Three is for
the lover's triangle, sadly
gone awry, that honey blonde
upon the witness stand,
swearing not to lie.

Four is for
half brothers, bickering
over the will, each one blaming
the other for slipping their
old Dad a pill.

Five is for
these ornate caskets,
resting all in a row, a week after
the shoot out down at Luigi's;
five mobsters, cold to go.

Six is for his
revolver, tossed into the center
of a lake, all six chambers empty,
the widow Robinson sipping
margaritas at his wake.

Seven is for
those classic deadly sins, and a
movie based thereon, a copycat killer
impatient in the wings, cooped
up for far too long.

Eight is for the
weekend hunters, stranded in their
mountain retreat, blizzard outside,
worst in a century, each one
desperate for fresh meat.

Nine is for the
sisters of mercy, young nurses
all dressed in white, stalked by
a knife wielding maniac, his
longings dark as night.

Ten is for old
Agatha's Indians, cleverly
dispatched one at a time, one little, two little
Indians, to fans of classic mystery,
a very familiar rhyme.

Eleven is for
that famous hour, when repricves
can save the day, except for Joe "the axe"
MacDougal, daylight savings somehow
forgotten along the way.

Twelve is for the
dozen jurors deliberating
behind closed doors, the repeat offender
before them, a video presence in one
too many convenience stores.

Thirteen is for this
baker's dozen, debauchery and
murder quite low, these crimes of passion,
psychopathy, and premeditation, all
equal on murderer's row.

Restaurant Tale

Carried away
by the restaurant's
ambiance,

he failed to notice
the chicken bone,

and soon left in
the back of a silent
ambulance.

Lamp

Moon so full tonight
the dead can read by its light
tales of the living.

Uninvited Guest

After the sun sinks,
the sea turns primordial black
and full fathom cold,

icy stars marking the break
between deep, dark water and
infinite night.

Horizon bound, a ship full
of passengers eating, drinking and
making merry,

unaware of the ancient
thing stirring deep beneath their
barnacle studded hull,

down where light goes to die,
and nightmare rarities pin their prey
in cold phosphorescent glow.

Gay dance music, a Strauss
waltz, filters down to that other
world, distorted by the depth

and makeup of the water,
the vibrations unnerving some,
their hunt momentarily

interrupted by alien sounds,
defenses heightened, all but the
Master of their realm.

G. O. Clark

Undeterred by such things,
his dully glowing tentacles waving
about in time to the music,

he prepares for a trip to the
surface, the replenishment of air,
and a freshly set buffet.

Fear

The stars
are light-daggers
to those who've
lost focus,

the moon
a leprous face
peering out of
the fog,

the universe
an endless night
teeming with
dark delusions.

The Stranger

The stranger sets off
car alarms when he stalks
the midnight streets; a shrill
warning to some.

Passing through
the cemetery, he pauses to
sharpen his long, black nails
on the granite tombstones.

Each night he seeks out
darkened bedroom windows,
avoiding those still lit by
late night TV glow.

His prey is always the
same. Young, female, asleep
and dreaming of prom dresses
and athletic young men.

Come the morning,
a parent's worst nightmares
become real, sheets stained red
with shattered dreams.

The stranger come and
gone. Drained batteries, angry
commuters, death and sirens
left in his wake.

Only On Dying Lips

Everywhere she walks,
she's followed by dry leaves,
Fall leaves gone to parchment.

Every place she visits,
alarm clocks set at bedtime go
unchallenged come the morning.

Anyone she touches,
suddenly grows in their bones,
the future outstripped by their past.

Every time she smiles,
Winter spreads across the land,
and the wind shrieks like harpies.

Some call her Lady Death.
Others the Bride of Oblivion. Only
dying lips form her true name.

Sailing with the Devil

The Devil's sailboat
has eternally flaming sails,
and his crew members
take turns at being crucified
upon its razor sharp prow;
living figureheads
painfully pointing the way ahead
through blood stained eyes.

The Beast stands tall beside
the great tiller made of
broken and twisted human bones,
scrimshaw depictions of the damned
carved along its length,
steering a true course through
the sea of lost souls
towards the never setting sun.

The wake of His boat
is littered with the bloated,
severed limbs of the gray skinned dead,
anorexic carrion birds feeding
upon their remains,
the fetid air filled with sad laments
of the damned and the birds
hysterical squawking.

The lucky few,
fallen angels one and all,
get to lounge upon the sailboats deck,
traveling first class on this cruise,
acting out their sordid thoughts upon the
crew members and each other,
and patiently listening
to old Lucifer's twisted tales.

This Part of Town

In this part of town
when the street lights blink on
they bathe the sidewalks in shadow
instead of light.

As twilight bleeds into darkness,
the nameless stir beneath stiletto stars.

In this part of town
the taverns quickly fill after sundown,
shapes materializing from bar room smoke,
drinks on the house for the unwary.

As the moon cuts a swath through
the Milky Way, the screaming intensifies.

In this part of town
the women hide their souls in snakeskin
coin purses, and store the faintly beating hearts
of old lovers in hat boxes.

As a cacophony of clocks toll the witching hour,
fish-head-toting alley cats slink homeward.

In this part of town,
stray rivulets of blood seep into the
sidewalk cracks, as workaday normality returns
with the rising sun.

The Head

The head in the refrigerator,
in among the leftovers, condiments
and bottles of soda, doesn't
belong there.

There are no other body parts.
The arms and legs gone their own way.
The torso perhaps floating away
on some river's current.

The head is that of a male.
Middle aged, black hair, clean shaven.
Skin a pale shadow of the original.
Dead, gray eyes frozen open.

Nobody knows how it got there,
why it was left behind to begin with,
or who the poor fellow could possibly be.
Debate continues on what to do next.

So there it sits like rotting cheese,
waiting for someone to claim it, ready
for your deathly scream when you raid
the fridge for a little midnight snack.

G. O. Clark

Ghosts Of Dead Children

The ghosts of dead children
haunt school playgrounds, sand lot
ball fields, and amusement
park rides.

The ghosts of dead children
linger at Thanksgiving dinner card tables,
family picnics at the lakeshore, and
on lunchroom benches.

The ghosts of dead children
hide the toys of the living, shiny metal
trucks and rosy cheeked dolls,
come Christmas eve.

The ghosts of dead children
tap out spelling bee answers in the wee
hours of the night, their siblings stone
deaf to their coaching.

The ghosts of dead children
hover above their sleeping parents,
shielding them from recurring nightmares
and quicksand traps of sadness.

The ghosts of dead children
cling close to their Earthly homes,
tethered to their short-changed memories
and the warmth of the living.

Seasons of the Living Dead

Come spring
the snow pack melts
and the zombies thaw out,
picking up where they left off
before the winter freeze.

Summertime
is hard on decaying bodies,
the strongest sunscreen no longer
an option, sunglasses useless,
swimwear a bloody joke.

In autumn
the leaves turn, days grow
shorter, nights cooler and the
living dead perform their gruesome
tricks for bloody treats.

Winter brings
huddled nights by the fire,
burnt out Christmas lights, off-key
zombie carolers in the distance, and an
empty toast to the New Year.

Zombie Clowns

Zombie clowns
are the worst with their
bulbous red noses, floppy,
over-sized cartoon shoes,
mop-like orange hair
and baggy clothes.

Blood stained,
makeup smeared, tripping
over their own feet, mindlessly
miming forgotten things,
the dark street is their ring,
the night, ringmaster.

Players in your
walking dead nightmare,
they stand out like day-glow
balloons in a cemetery, pleasant
memories of circuses past
forgotten at first bite.

Zombie On A Leash

Like a stiff legged dog
on a leash

she's yanked this way
and that,

a post-mortem slave of
circumstance

bound to her master, her
pimp,

a decaying pleasure doll
sold into the

cold embrace of some
faceless necrophiliac.

Zombie Loner

He stands alone,
ragged and bent,
separate from the pack,
even in death
belonging nowhere.

The traditional
zombies, victims
of the voodoo curse,
are cliquish,
not open to new members.

The radioactive,
alien infested zombies -
hostages to the invisible -
have no say
as to who gets an invite.

The plague victim
zombies don't care who
rots with them, but his
immune system is too strong,
even long dead.

So he stumbles
through death alone,
feared by those still living,
ostracized by the dead,
odd man out
in a world gone mad.

Writer's Block

Staring at
the blank sheet of white
typing paper poking out of the
old Olympics' platen,

he doesn't have a clue
what to do, how to do it, or why,
the terrible hunger pains all he
can think about.

Being a famous writer has
lost all its glamour since becoming
one of them; body rotting away,
fans a mindless mob.

The critics no longer exist.
Deadlines are a thing of the past.
And the major literary award he won,
only serves as a bludgeon now.

G. O. Clark

Albino

The albino zombie
finds that fresh blood
adds rouge to his cheeks,
and no longer feels like
an outsider, accepted as is
by his fellow living dead.

It doesn't matter
that the same folks who
once considered him a freak
are now bent on chopping off
his pink eyed, white haired,
deathly pale head.

He's all zombie now,
dead to the behind-his-back
whisperings of strangers
and friends alike, done with
the old pretenses of society,
the past a total blank.

Rag Doll

Little Jill
got left behind with
nothing but the clothes on
her back, and a rag doll.

Now little Jill
blindly wanders the
streets and back alleys, totally
lost, and forgetful.

Little Jill has been
shot twice, run over by a car,
and fallen off a bridge, but still
keeps shuffling along.

The 2012 Pandemic
stole little Jill's childhood,
wiped her mind clean of cartoons
and ice cream dreams.

Little Jill imitates
the mindless actions of her elders,
following the pack from one
fresh kill to another.

Poor little Jill, bloody
rag doll clutched in her tiny
dead hand, warm blood replacing
Kool-Aid as her favorite drink.

Reanimated

Cartoon zombies
have taken over the
towns and cities of the
real world.

Betty Boop
stumbles along like
a bloody bobble head,
spring all but shot.

Mickey and Minnie
fight over the remains
of Pluto, ripping at his flesh
like starving hyenas.

Bugs Bunny
gnaws on Elmer Fudd's
dismembered arm as if it
were a fresh carrot.

Rocky and Bullwinkle
work as a team; moose
cornering the meat, squirrel
dive-bombing the brains.

The Flintsones,
Jetsons, Simpsons and
the Family Guy's brood all
real as Roger Rabbit,

reanimated by some
deity's twisted sense of humor,
end of the world a crazed
Looney Tune nightmare.

Two Drink Minimum

The zombie audience
mimics the motions of the
living, their dead eyes reflecting
the flickering candles
upon the tables,

as the dark haired,
rose lipped cabaret singer,
bathed by a blood red spotlight,
performs her world weary,
sultry song,

playing to those
long forgotten impulses,
mutated dreams, and impotent
Viagra blues of the
living dead,

this final night
of the human species
spreading across the dying Earth
like a long, drawn out,
toxic breath.

Scarecrow

Its brain
is made of straw,
its clothes torn, dirty rags
loosely hung upon a
rib-less body,

its eyes,
empty sockets,
its mouth stitched closed,
and its nonsectarian crucifixion
a cobbled together affair

witnessed
by a zombie priest,
kneeling in the corn field,
clerical collar speckled with blood,
gazing ever heavenward.

G. O. Clark

Some Zombies One Should Avoid

Zombie politicians -
who linger over your brain,
take forever to finish their task,
then shake your limp hand in the end.

Salesmen zombies -
who push their mindless sales pitch
upon you, crowding your front door and
trashing your living room carpet if
given the chance.

Evangelical zombies -
who act blankly determined to
save your soul, to convert you to their
fuzzy belief systems and twisted visions
of eternity.

Radio talk show zombies -
who babble on throughout the night
to their half-conscious listeners, the later
willfully offering up their gray matter
to irrational half-truths.

Corporate zombies -
who march around in expensive,
but tattered business suits, flailing their
MBA's in your face, determined to drag
you down to their bottom line.

Finally, zombie relatives -
those you haven't seen for years,
those who repeatedly sponge off you,
and those who literally interpret the proverb,
blood is thicker than water, intent on
draining you of every last drop.

The Last Zombie

The last zombie on Earth
doesn't feel alone,
has no concept of its isolation,
pines for no one.

It still has a relentless appetite
for fresh brains,
but the competition is zilch
since becoming the last zombie.

In the abandoned, silent city
the last zombie stumbles
into nothing living or dead, not even
a stray cat or dog.

The last zombie will eventually
get hunted down,
a bullet to the head, or fire axe to its
muddled brain.

The survivors of the plague
will eventually spread tall tales about
the last zombie on Earth,
twisting the facts about its lineage.

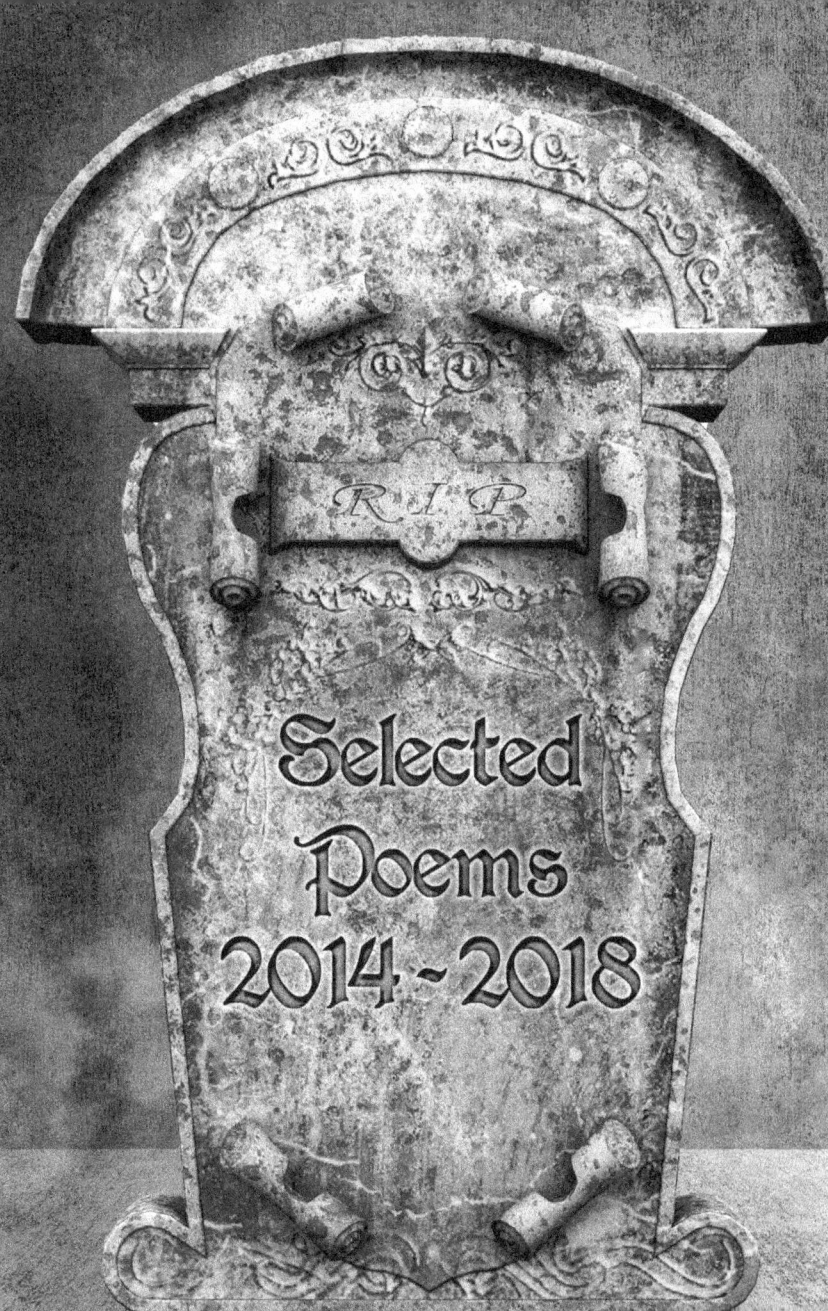

The Party Crashers Scenario

Six werewolves
pulling a blood-red carriage,
nobody at the reins,

Count Dracula
inside with three of his brides,

speeding through
the black forest below a crimson
moon,

all their pulses throbbing,
all their appetites unsatisfied;

destination, another
all-night rave at some billionaire's
ancestral castle,

invitations taken at the door
by the moonlighting mortician

out to mingle with the rich,
leer at the coeds, and graciously
offer up his services at night's end.

The Darkness Within

There's a darkness tonight
darker than the unformed mind
of a month old fetus,

darker than a vein of coal
buried deep beneath the tranquil
West Virginia hill,

darker than the soul of the
serial killer, his twisted fantasies
playing out in real-time,

darker than the space beyond
the edge of the known universe,
beyond imagination's reach.

There's a darkness tonight
dragging its fingernails across the
dusty blackboard of my soul,

obliterating the dream of pure light.

G. O. Clark

The White Sedan

On my daily
bike ride through this old
cemetery, twilight just
descending,

I spy the owls
taking flight from their
perches atop the hilltop trees,
heading

out for their
nightly hunt, silently
circling and drifting towards
the nearby rooftops.

The evening air has
lost its afternoon warmth,
the headstones releasing their
stony coldness.

It's too early
for ghosts, but not those
twilight wanderers who appear
come sundown,

creeping forth from their
dusty abodes to walk among
the graves: souls in limbo,
waiting for closure.

As I pedal on,
not wanting to linger,
I keep my distance from the old
white sedan backed

into one path's dead end,
parked in the same spot each night,
bathed in soot and shadows,
engine idling.

The white sedan
with that hulking figure
hunched over its steering wheel,
patiently waiting

for the already dead,
or perhaps a stray bicyclist.
Lurking there again in the shadows
as I quickly head

towards the gate,
pedaling faster, stiletto-like
fingernails tapping upon my spine,
hurrying away from the dead

towards the relative
safety of the rooftops, and
the routine business of the owls
on a mouse-wary night.

Dark Forest

In a forest
that has never enjoyed
sunlight,

the trees,
shrubs and lady slippers
are tinted black.

In a forest
nourished each night by
filtered moonlight,

blood-lustful
creatures silently stalk their
pale prey.

In a forest,
leafy canopied and dripping
with moon dew,

two shadows
huddle as one against the
primordial darkness,

the scent of their blood,
and pounding of their hearts,
beacons in the night.

A Stone Angel's Tears

The sound of the
stone angel's wings lifting
her off her perch echoes
in the night.

The busy worms
burrow deep below her,
slithering among the rib cages
of the freshly interred.

The moon sends out
blue wavelengths of sadness
that penetrate her rigidity
and headstones alike.

And now in flight,
the angel surveys her domain,
a last hint of smoke from
the crematorium

drifting her way,
the whisper of some recently
cremated soul brushing past
her stone ear,

her long night soon
to give way to another day
of black-dress ceremony, and
fresh marble tears.

Head Games

She collects shrunken heads;
old high school beaus,
Johnny, Billy, Jim and Biff.

Her former husbands, Ned, Ted,
Tom and Fred,

plus college professors,
Mr.'s Chambers, Delgado and Chan,

and those lascivious bosses,
Benson, Templeton, and McSweeny.

The eyes and lips of each head are
permanently stitched shut.

The size of each head, a near-perfect
fit to her tannin-stained hands.

The dark story behind each trophy,
far too long for this poem.

She collects shrunken heads,
and is quite comfortable
in her own alabaster skin.

The Taste of Death

She loved cooking gourmet,
and his appetite had no bounds.

It was gastronomic bliss for him.

She was a true expert in the use
of seasonings and extracts.

Sweet or sour, his taste buds sang.

As for poisons, she only used them
sparingly, to prolong his agony.

He never Googled the warning signs.

Their culinary bliss lasted many years,
until her fatal car accident.

There was speculation upon the cause.

He lived to age ninety, his last words,
her cooking was to die for.

If Only the Leaves Could Talk

The leaves remember that night,
the full moon, the mist, the screams,
the muddy boots crushing their fallen
numbers in the dark, empty park.

The leaves recall the body
of the screaming girl thrashing about
atop their fallen numbers, their Fall finest
drenched with her warm blood.

The leaves couldn't protest when
their fallen numbers were crudely used to
conceal her ravaged body, the killer
cursing all things fragile.

The leaves just did what they
always do, scatter upon the wind and
await the surly gardener and his blower;
tread of patent-leather shoes to come.

The Lost Maiden's Secrets

In a bark canoe,
resting askew upon
the dry, exposed river rocks
of the old riverbed,

from an age long past
when every forest was enchanted,
and river, liquid magic,

a maiden out of time,
dressed in faded silk finery,
bejeweled with turquoise and gold,

hollow eye sockets
filled with ghostly tears,
her long bony fingers clasping
an ornate, locked diary.

Ghost Coda

The sound
of her pale withered hands
clapping, clapping,
clapping,

in the darkness
of the grand old opera house,

the cultured and elite audience
fading away into the foggy
city night,

blood red curtains drawn,
diva, orchestra, conductor and crew
off to recoup before the next
performance,

the dust of years settling back down
upon the darkened stage

leaving behind in the dark vacuum
the sound of her pale withered hands
clapping, clapping,
clapping,

her disembodied hold
upon that special night so long ago,

her lone-ghost standing ovation
repeated every night at
performance end;

pale, withered hands clapping,
clapping, clapping,
clapping....

The Waiting Shadows

She keeps the shadows
of her youth in a steamer trunk,
stowed away in the attic.

The shadows of her college
Days are pressed between the pages
of her secret diary.

Her children's shadows
lay hidden beneath the photographs in
dust covered family albums.

The shadow of her husband
hangs in the closet with his shirts, suits,
and blood-stained bathrobe.

Throughout the house lurk
their dark shadows, each one stuck
in limbo along with her own, waiting
for a new family to move in.

Preserves

In her basement,
across from the old coal
burning furnace,

thirteen shelves
of home canned goods
from the garden.

Summer vegetables,
preserved for Winter tables.
Jams and jellies aplenty.

Perfectly pickled
rodents, frogs, birds and
long lost pets.

She's expert at canning
the shallow rooted: the warm
and cold-blooded.

Her best-of-show
rest upon some special shelves
back in the shadows:

human fetuses
abandoned by her coven
sisters, sealed and

saved for the Master,
his aborted progeny preserved
in the cellar cold.

G. O. Clark

The Sea Monster

When the sea monster
casually walked out of the waves,
it took all the weekenders on the beach
by total surprise.

It was one of those flat-wave kind of days.

At first they thought it
was an optical illusion. Then they looked
around for the film crew and director.
Finally, they realized it was real.

Strange that none of them had a camera.

But by then it was too late!
Their yapping dogs became appetizers!
Their obese, candy filled kids, got gobbled up!
And the rest became its meat and potatoes.

It had stiletto sharp teeth and a giant appetite.

Fully sated, the creature burped, and
tail wagging, sauntered back into the waves,
the beach in its wake littered with bloody props
for the Six O'clock News.

Gravediggers' Dance

The gravediggers
swirl around
the cold tombstones,
their dance floor, dewy grass,
full moon a chandelier,
the music of life
filling the pulseless silence
and nibbling at their ears,
the buried dead below
keeping time with boney toes,
and silently perched
above their moonlit revelry,
the chaperone angel,
her curfew cast in stone.

Endgame

He thought
if he just sat perfectly still,
Death would blindly pass him by.

She thought
by painting all her mirrors black,
Time would never be reflected again.

Together they made
quite a couple, cowering from the future,
inside their dust covered past.

Time can pass through doors and walls
The Future is ever patient.
Death never gives up.

Parting Shots

She mailed
a massive funnel cloud to her
abusive ex-husband.

He had a very stormy personality.

She FedExed the
vengeful ghost of a prostitute
to her former boss.

He'd treated her like one for years.

She shipped via UPS
a Lovecraftian god-monster to her
Catholic school Alma Mata.

The sadistic nuns had it coming.

She wasn't a vengeful person.
Nor was she born evil, Satan's little
mistress, or, delusional.

She'd been baptized, and psychoanalyzed.

She was just taking a few parting shots
before retiring to the cloistered woods,
and the bylaws of the coven.

It was her turn to bring snacks.

Redeye

In this city
come the night,
all the women look
beautiful, and the men
handsome.

The streets glow
with a soft amber light,
the cafes fill with whispers,
and the air is thick with
exotic aromas.

From the rooftops
lift the strains of some
ancient music, waking the
gargoyles from their stony
sleep to dance.

Surrounding the
city, the forest seethes,
extremes of dark imagining
taking shape, the hour of
feasting drawing near.

On this night
terrible things transpire,
the mauling of flesh and bone
but a prequel to the spread
of madness come dawn.

Visitors to the city,
those who survive, relate
tales of carnage in the streets,
viewed safely from their
hotel windows;

the beautiful women
and handsome men helpless
against grotesque, crazed things,
all claws and flashing teeth,
hunting them below.

In a plane flying over
the city, you'd never guess
what was occurring far beneath
your pressurized safety, the lights
below like any other city

spied from on high,
until a gargoyle, not really
keen on dancing, lands on the
wing, and your screams join in
with those far below.

The Comfort Of Screams

The distant screams
lull him to sleep each night.

They're a dark form of hope;
others targeted instead of him.

At first the city was
filled with non-stop screaming,

a million souls being
systematically slaughtered like sheep.

As the ravenous things spread,
the screams became more sporadic,

the blood-stained streets
deserted; fresh kills more random.

Before the blackout, FOX News declared,
Earth's become one big smorgasbord!

Dreams filled with PG-rated ET's,
have been replaced by hellish nightmares.

The dying screams of others
lull him to sleep, high up in his penthouse,

safe for now from the nightmare source
of the human extinction event.

Postcard From The Night Desert

Late at night, the bats
suck nectar from the saguaro cactuses,
like vampires from the necks
of prickly old maids.

Some fallen saguaros,
ribs highlighted by the full moon's glow,
litter the ground like dead vaqueros
after a barroom brawl.

Darkness, death and
things that slither dot the parched desert
landscape, along with tiny lizards dreaming
their velociraptor dreams.

Ancient eyes follow the
midnight tourist, tooth and claw eager
to tear into tender flesh; picked clean
skeleton left to bleach in the sun.

G. O. Clark

Nesting Habits Of The Mutant Crows

The last insult
to his wretched life
was the mutant crows
salvaging the small
bones from his fingers,
the same fingers he'd
made music with when
still alive and topping
the charts - guitar and soul
connected - the screams
of the audience now
replaced with loud cawing
and skeletal rattling;
the bones, *his bones*,
destined to become part
of the crow's gruesome
nests, high up in the
branches of some
post-apocalyptic tree,
the music of his world
gone deathly silent.

Her Apparition Walked Right Through Him

Her apparition walked right through him,
like smoke through a rusty screen door.

There was no spinal chill, nor sensation
of death clouding his old, tormented soul.

There *was* the sudden impact of memories,
good and bad, of their brief life together.

Their senior prom; her pink taffeta, his
tight cummerbund; his slow-dance arousal.

The sights and smells of the delivery room
drama; that first scream of many to follow.

The cold night outside her window, outside
her house, her mystery date warm inside.

The story on page two of the local newspaper:
"Divorcee still missing and feared dead".

Her apparition walked right through him,
frigid as ice, heavy as a granite tombstone.

Scents Upon A Delta Breeze

She left the window open
on those warm summer nights,
to cool her bedroom, to smell the
the scent of flowers cooling after
a long day beneath the sun.

Roses in full bloom.
Tendrils of Star Jasmine
spreading into the nearby Ivy.
The natural border of Rosemary
bushes, favored by the bees.

Night after night the
scents reach her, envelope her
as she falls asleep; distant sounds
of trains and freeway traffic mixing
with crickets and hushed voices.

Summer after summer
the pattern repeated; open window,
cool breeze, scents and sounds, right
up to the night Death dropped by;
as sermonized by her priest,

prognosticated by her doctor,
and sanctioned by Time. Death appeared
smelling of rotten vegetables, road kill
decay, and fresh corpses supine
upon the autopsy table.

Death came to lead her and
others away that night, their beds
emptied of all vitality, their voices
hushed, the scent of summer blooms
drifting toward the cemetery.

A Tale Of Blood & Gasoline

The killer car
parks wherever it pleases;
handicap space, beside a fire
hydrant, loading zone, even a
freeway car-pool lane.

Tow trucks give it
a wide birth, police cars
go limp and slink away, and
18-wheelers know better than
to cross its path.

There's no one sentient
behind the killer car's wheel.
It has a mind of its own filled
with machine coldness and
classic road rage.

Wartime carnage pales
next to the mass destruction
left in its wake; the collateral
damage within its sphere,
merciless and total.

The killer car is painted
blood-red, has a high decibel
horn that mimics Cthulhu in heat,
and Dagmar bumpers honed
to a stiletto sharpness.

Everything on two or more
legs is fair game, its favorite
hunting grounds community parks,
weekend shopping malls, and
church parking lots.

Songs will be written about
the killer car, muscle cars adopt
its missing-muffler growl, and its
reign of terror continue until every
drop of blood and gas is gone.

Dark Angels Descending

The dark angels' wings
are made of fragile things
stitched together;

parchments and silks,
prayers and wishes,
flesh and feather.

The wings extended
spread eternal darkness
across the land,

the fire and brimstone
ravings of TV evangelists
finally proving true.

The clanging
of the Armageddon bells
pierce one's sanity,

as human DNA
unravels and wall calendars
burst into flame.

Our mass extinction is
not so much an event, as a
cosmic afterthought lost in
the vastness of time.

Cthulhu's Checklist

Claws -- check.
Wings -- check.
Tentacles -- check.
Glowing eyes -- check.
2000 decibel,
bone shattering,
blood curdling, mind
numbing ROAR -- check.
Briny, mutilated
corpse smell -- check.
Pass-key to a forgotten
time -- check.
Parallel universe
coordinates -- check.
Sit wherever I want
attitude -- check.
Big bag of kick-ass
mania – check!

G. O. Clark

The Mortician's Daughter

The mortician's daughter
loves to play with her dolls,
inviting them to afternoon tea,
packing them into an antique
perambulator for long walks in
the park, and brushing their long,
silky hair, counting each stroke
with a tiny, sing-song voice.

The mortician loves his
daughter, more than anything
in the world, yet often fears her
as well. Her dark power to change
inanimate things into living, breathing
abominations strains his heart. Those
dolls of hers with their blank, staring
eyes and secretive whispers behind
his back, taunt his tired soul.

His daughter is like any
normal blue-eyed, blond-haired
little girl. Her home not unlike other
ones, despite being a mortuary. Her aunt
took the place of her deceased mother, home
schooling her niece in the basics, and skills
more esoteric. Forbidden arts handed down
from mother to daughter; stealing of souls
from the recently deceased a specialty.

The mortician's daughter still
loves her dolls, even post puberty
when the new additions to her growing
collection began having names like Ken,
Damien and even Raymond, after her father,
who still goes about his routine of preparing
the recently deceased for interment, the eyes
of her dolls no longer haunting him, their
whispers full-voiced in his head; his
unblinking eyes, now doll-like.

Rock On

Fender Strat in boney hand,
he plays riffs with amazing ease
and agility, the bones in his fingers
stretching their fleshly bounds

to caress the metal strings
like wire-thin throats, to wring
the notes out of them and make them
scream with ear-piercing pleasure.

Some say the Strat keeps
him alive, funnels the electricity
directly into his nerves, and then
his aging, burnt out brain.

A real dead head, no longer
clinically alive, he left reality behind
back in the Sixties; the music press,
then as now, labeling him a zombie.

He's electrifying on stage,
gyrating to the groove, all fluidity
and jangling bones until the plug gets
pulled and the lights dim.

No groupie is crazy enough
to seek his bones by the stage door,
their traditional free-love lifestyle
not necrophiliac inclusive.

G. O. Clark

Hitchhiker

A hitchhiking clown late for
his next appearance, balloon strings
clutched in his white gloved left hand,
thumb on right hand extended towards
the speeding traffic, beckoning to
the weekend travelers.

Your kids want you to stop
and pick him up, multi-colored
balloons reflected in their bright eyes.
Your wife wants you to pass him by,
already mad at you for not leaving
on time for the movie.

As for you? You're conflicted.

Ignore your wife, which will
have consequences later in bed; please
the kids, which will be construed as more
spoiling on your part; or heed the memory
of Killer Clowns From Outer Space
and Stephen King's, IT.

Erring on the side of caution,
you speed on by, the clown framed
in your rear view mirror lowering his
thumb and raising his middle finger,
sun glinting off the tip of a blood
stained butcher knife poking out
of one baggy, red sleeve.

Corn Maze

Some go into the corn maze
intent on winning the game,
on proving their inner compass
better than most.

High school couples go in
to scare one another, cuddle and
kiss, and escape from their
parents prying eyes.

Kids go in with matinee
fears, nervous laughter and tears,
briefly putting their terror aside
to ditch their parents.

Old folks go into the maze
to relive Halloween memories from
their youth, and sneer at those
clichés about old age.

Others go in to hunt, season
open, the scent of human blood fresh
in their nostrils; jack-o-lanterns
sardonically smiling outside.

G. O. Clark

The Coroner

He dismantles the dead,
surgically removing their
internal organs, lifting out
their lifeless brains like an
obstetrician gently guiding
out another newborn.

With scalpel and saw
he performs his autopsies
with practiced precision,
the deceased feeling no pain,
the ticking clock on the wall
drowned out by his clinical
voice describing each stage
of the post-mortem exam.

If only the dead knew
the truth, the secret he's
lived with since childhood
when he performed his first
autopsy, playing that classic
Operation game, patient's
red nose lighting up when
his skill with tweezers
got a bit too sloppy.

He always played by
himself, but curing the
patient's broken heart, water
on the knee, or butterflies in
the stomach was irrelevant.
He just loved taking the patient

apart and not putting him back
together again. The only fee for
his services, morbid fun.

He visualizes the game
each time he dismantles a
fresh corpse, waiting for its
nose to light up when he falters
removing a 45 slug, silent heart,
or warm brain with its fading
grasp upon reality; the job is just
a simple game to him, one he'll
always win in the end.

Postmortem Regret

A thin layer of ash from
the fires of Hell coats his classic
50's Buick Roadmaster each morn.

The car is his pride and joy,
and what with water rationing,
its become hard to keep it pristine.

Folks warned him about living
downwind from the core, but he wanted
to live close to the action.

On any given night he can hear
screams of agony and cacophonous
music off in the distance,

and when he leaves his bedroom
window open, the smell of barbecue
drifts in to temp his taste buds.

When he retired, and involuntarily
had to downsize, his only options were
the fringes of Hell, or, suburbs of Heaven.

He chose Hell of course,
more adventurous then most his age;
adverse to white clothes, regardless of style.

He accepts his post-mortem lot,
weird neighbors and all, but regrets not
having packed a tarp for the Roadmaster.

Cataclysm

It happened
in a flash,
the twinkle taken
out of the stars,

the planet's atmosphere
ripped away, everything
vacuum bound;

one great cloud
of hopes and dreams,
wars and schemes

cast into space as if
gravity suddenly just grew
tired of the whole damn thing.

At The Spa

The once famous Blob,
now completely neutralized,
works in the mud baths.

The Unraveling

The classic Mummy
unraveling in the end,
dust to dust again.

Leisureville

One doesn't walk
around here after dark,
aware of the pulse beats of beasts
unseen lurking in the bushes,
tree branches overhead notched
by the claws of deadly raptors,
their reptile brains primed for
carrion slaughter.

One stays home,
doors and windows locked,
avoiding the garrulous gnomes,
pale plaster angels with broken
wings, hungry Halloween skulls,
and the blood stained shovels, rakes,
hoes, tomato trellis traps and
other garden club tools of torture,
waiting in the shadows of the sheds
to prune and pulverize.

One doesn't linger
outside the darkened windows
of these tomb-like mobile homes
that line the circular streets and
pathways, divorced from the world
at large, midnight marking the time
of open season upon insomniacs out for
moonlit strolls; trigger happy, wary seniors
defending their final leases on life against
old nightmares, childhood born;
never forgotten.

Caged Fear

The thing in the cage
is invisible, mute, and smells
like nothing of this Earth.

We feed it twice a day
with the raw meat of our
imaginations, and the moisture
of fearful anticipation.

A while back the cage door
was carelessly left open overnight,
and the next morning we found
bloody paw prints from its
comings and goings.

The morning papers were
filled with headlines about
unexplained deaths, mutilated
corpses, and nightmares
now become real.

The police never traced
the perpetrator to our secret,
sub-basement labs. Why it chose
to return after one day of freedom,
still remains a mystery.

New locks now adorn
its cage, and 24 hour video
camera surveillance has added
an extra measure of security.

G. O. Clark

We made an example
of the lab assistant responsible
for absent mindedly setting the
thing free; the fact it's invisible,
not a valid excuse.

His family has been
duly notified and received
generous compensation for
their loss. The official cause
of death; lab accident.

His fellow employees
were required to view his
mangled remains, as an object
lesson. It's worked so far.

We still don't know
what we're dealing with,
other than the fact it has four
sharp claws, and is prone to
indiscriminant slaughter.

The blood from its
murderous night out proved to
be that of its victims, human and
animal, leaving us no genetic
clue to its phylum, or origin.

A dark, palpable presence,
it silently lurks behind the cage
bars; nightmare made real.

Weeds

She's emaciated,
all of five feet tall,
her stringy hair a mix
of gray and dish-water brown,
her face a field of life-long
smoker's wrinkles, surmounted
by old horn rimmed glasses held
together by Scotch tape.

She wanders around
the senior park seemingly
lost to reality, sometimes trying
to start up conversations,
only to lose her train of thought
and wander off to the trailer
she calls home; her mad husband
quarantined in the shadows,
behind discolored blinds.

She's the nemesis of weeds,
randomly tidying up yards along
her route; crab grass, dandelions,
thistles, all manner of intrusive
vegetation picked clean by
 her small, unwashed hands and
deposited in handy garbage cans;
home owners unaware, or more likely,
just not giving a damn.

She was once a petite,
pretty girl who early on got
worn down by life's random chaos;

a fragile child grown to womanhood,
victim of destructive relationships,
bad luck, and psychiatric misdiagnosis;
pumped full of pills and left by the
curb; another dead soul
weeded out and forgotten.

A Darker Shade Than Normal

Pandemic bound,
I pass the hours doing
long delayed Spring cleaning,
the dust of what seems ages,
finally tackled;

cliché bunnies
hidden under the beds,
books of all sizes blown on
and rubbed with a soft cloth,
shelves dusted.

The dust has built up
over the years, accumulating
while I was traveling or at work,
filling nooks and crannies,
shrouding dead insects.

A year, going on two,
of self isolation, compulsive
housework, and thoughts of death,
avoiding that one dusty corner,
a darker shade than normal.

G. O. Clark

A Very Limited Engagement

Cirque Du Soleil's
very limited engagement
performance of their
Homage To H.P. Lovecraft,
sold out within minutes.

The initial ad stated that
triage would be set up in the
venue parking lots beforehand,
for all those who survive.

Reviews are still pending.

Hoping For A Menu Change

Sitting on her porch,
knitting an intricate spider web,
the old witch pays close attention
to all that passes by.

Her wrinkled hands deftly
ply the knitting needles, the
clicking sounds in sync with those
of her eight arthritic knee joints,
cozy warm beneath the quilt her
mother sewed and tucked her
in with when little.

She's the definition
of patience, always attentive to
her prey, but lacking much appetite
for the usual fare of plump little puppies,
unattended babies asleep in their strollers,
and random park bench squatters
trying to recall their yesterdays.

Knit and stitch, knit
and stitch, her web expanding;
the hunger building for something
new and truly exotic.

A Hole In The Dark

There's a hole
in the dark out there,
beyond the porch light,
a mystery begging
to be solved.

It's not a mini
black hole, scientists
confirm, nor the door to
Hell according to
the priests.

It passively waits
for a child's imagination,
an adult's fearful paranoia,
or this aging man's
retrospection.

It's just
a hole in the dark,
out beyond my porch light,
everything and nothing
encompassing all.

Of Wood Chippers & Band Saws

The chainsaws
are busy this morning,
dead limbs and live chewed
on by their oil-smeared
steel teeth.

Was that a scream I heard
in the middle of all the noise?

There's a lot of old trees
around the neighborhood;
oaks, elms, palms, evergreens,
cherished by most, a bother
to the few.

That definitely sounded like a
scream between the saw cuts.

The men, Mexican
laborers, short in stature,
muscular, shimmy up the trunks
with care, or proficiently
pilot the cherry picker.

Can't the workers hear
the same screams that I hear?

Nearly finished now,
lunchtime approaching, they
feed the cut branches into the
wood chipper, its terrifying
sound felt in my bones.

G. O. Clark

The screams have finally stopped;
the wood chipper gone silent.

Job done, the crew leaves,
my day back to the normal duet
of traffic noise and bird song; the
whine of my next door neighbor's
band saw firing up..

A Smell Of Coffee And Sulfur

Coffee in hand,
I checked my spam
folder this morning and
found a total of 666
emails waiting.

Most of them
were Phishing attempts
after my personal info,
or ads for various male
libido enhancers.

There was also a
slew of requests for
donations to the Home
For Unwed Witches, and,
Satan's Kids Home.

I experienced
a tug at my heart
strings for the later,
but burnt in the past,
deleted every last spam.

The smell of sulfur,
and the electric shock
I immediately got from
my keyboard, must mean
my old PC is now cursed,
and, time to upgrade.

G. O. Clark

Leaving The Past Behind

She putts the shrunken head
with her blood-red croquet mallet,
it striking the other heads with gusto,
the final bone-wicket her goal;
another win, game over.

She plays alone this moonlit
night, the mansion's backyard playing
course empty but for her, and familiar
family ghosts wandering back and
forth along the sidelines.

She silently glides forward,
Full-length black satin dress with
scarlet colored trim the color of her
hair, flowing across the grass like
a fully sentient fog.

The croquet game was a solemn
tradition, played at gatherings of the
clan on Halloween, the solstices, and
birthdays, the leathery shrunken heads
former slaves and husbands.

This night she's not celebrating
anything other than the peace and
quiet of aloneness, the empty hulking
mass of stone and wood behind her
locked up for the last time,

the skeleton chauferred 1930's
Bentley idling out front by the dry,
weed filled fountain; midnight ticking
ever closer, the open road ahead
snaking into the future.

As the clocks in the darkened
estate strike midnight, she takes her
final shot, husband number thirteen's
sullen shrunken head bashing twelve's
through the final boney wicket,

their silent screams muffled by
sewn tight lips, the ghosts of her ancestors
pausing long enough to turn their heads
and smile, and bid her goodbye with
whispered words and limp waves.

Slumped in the velvety back seat
of the Bentley, Mr. Melrose's boney
hands urging the steering wheel right and
left to navigate the winding driveway
down the ancestral mountain,

she spies the fiery glow of her
past framed in the rearview mirror,
sighs deeply, then turns on her I Phone,
three centuries behind her, the 21st
straight ahead in the darkness.

Oblivion's Realm

They met
by walking right through
one another, two ghosts
fresh from reality.

No handshakes
nor pats on the back.
No hugs or kisses on one
another's cheeks. Nothing solid
to grasp onto.

They both died
trekking along the same
path, same night, their hearts
not up to the strain.

It wasn't a cliché
dark and stormy night,
just a typical fall evening
with some scattered clouds
and a handful of stars.

Two strangers
meeting in the night,
their life's routines cut short;
time suddenly fuzzy.

They stopped,
they turned, they attempted
to communicate but soon realized
though one's lips moved, only
silence emerged.

After a few mimed
gestures, quizzical looks,
muted *good lucks,* and helpless
shrugs, they parted ways.

Time waits for no one,
even after death, and equally
resigned, they moved on
to oblivion's realm.

Dead Men Walking

This is the graveyard
of sunken dreams, failed schemes,
and grey/green broken timbers,
five fathoms deep,

corral tombstones abundant.

Ghost captains and crews
restlessly wandering about, water
sifting through their skeletons,
seaweed beards flowing,

the current animating faded flags

atop barnacled masts,
the ships taking on silt and sand,
cannons loaded with silence,
gold long ago scavenged.

And these dead men walking,
walking, eternally walking; shore
never drawing nearer, the sea
dead calm, air stagnant.

A Crime Of Passion

Look closely
at her eye, the dark iris,
that clock face pinned
dead center,

minute and hour hands
precisely stopped at midnight.

Listen intently
to her silent heart, the cold
absence of ticking,
pulse dead,

flow of blood slowed to nothing;
seat of emotions empty.

Step back
and see the bloody hammer
swung in anger in your
trembling hand,

it's claw-end incapable
of undoing one's raging passion.

Ghosts Of Christmas Past

The Christmas tree lights,
hanging from the cross beam,
are covered in dust and cobwebs,
Mrs. Havisham's ghost reclining
upon the couch below.

What is she doing here,
this fictional escapee from
my Victorian/Edwardian lit class;
the professor of which a fervent
Steampunk aficionado.

There's thousands of books
lining my living room, stuffed
full with ghosts real and fictional,
stoically waiting for a good dusting
and cracking of spines.

Who needs Scrooge to
remind us about Christmas spirit,
or Mrs. Havisham about the follies
of love, empty chairs, and
the silence of tears.

I gaze into the mirror,
and see my own ghost trapped
in the mists of uncertainty, victim
of a dark deed as yet to be discovered,
greeting card discarded,

my present caught in limbo,
past stored out of sight and mind,
future stalled between multiple realms.
A ghost without a clue, final chapter
hanging by a comma.

Tiny Houses Of The Forgotten

The abandoned cemetery
is covered with wildflowers,

orange poppies, dandelions,
lupines, miners lettuce and more.

Its grave markers, headstones, and
solidified angels forgotten by all

but the lingering ghosts, monk-like
ravens and the rats.

Its dozen or so mausoleums,
now tiny houses for the homeless,

ragtag skeletal survivors,
their conversations with the dead

echoing in the night, world outside
speeding by on cruise control.

The Arms Of Death

Is it the voices
of sirens or angels we hear
out there in the fog;

death upon the
rocks, or the warm embraces
of heavenly creatures.

Their voices beckoning,
do we dare draw any nearer,
ignore our compass,

lower our sails; the
coin suspended in mid toss
above the tiller?

Their hypnotic songs
are legend, tendrils of melody
tugging at our souls,

the last thing we sense
before our ship explodes into
splinters upon the rocks.

The songs of angels
are hymns of welcome to
the ethereal realm,

the siren's deadly tunes,
the flipside of the same record;
arms of death waiting.

G. O. Clark

Selfies

He was taking a selfie
when Leatherface fired up the
chainsaw behind him.

She was taking a selfie
when the Count photo-bombed
her final smart phone smile.

They were taking a selfie
when giant tentacles reached over
Pier 39's wooden railing.

I was taking a selfie
when my axe-wielding girlfriend
caught me kissing another.

We were all taking selfies
as the mushroom clouds bloomed
above our self-absorption.

Demon Weather

The wind gusts
whip around the house,
the wailing Banshee poised
outside oblivious to its
deadly effects.

Windows secure,
I cower like a little boy,
afraid of things in the dark,
the world outside busily going
about its daytime ritual.

Shingles are
lifting off the roof,
tree limbs slapping at the
walls, BB-like pebbles pinging
against the window glass.

To go outside
would be submission
to the blind forces of nature,
and that lady of darkness waiting
near the tree line.

The north wind is a
consequence of pressure
gradients, according to the
chief meteorologist on
the local news.

Doppler radar images,
computer generated maps,
professional attire and lame
predictions for the week ahead
dismiss my altered reality.

The power is out,
TV antenna air born, and
contact with the world cut off;
the politics of climate change
becoming too personal.

The wind will slowly
peel away the layers of my
house like those of an onion,
and with luck carry me off to OZ,
far from her demon embrace.

The Darkness Behind The Dark

There's a darkness
behind the dark, beyond the
scattered light of night,

a place where eyes
prove more than blind,
and the sense of touch and
smell don't exist.

A realm where
the ear overhears dark
whispers from things waiting
to be imagined, and

beasts of flesh and
blood and sentient skeletons
not of this world -- ravenous
appetites never sated --

wait in that darkness
behind the dark for lights out,
and REM sleep where bloody
nightmares hatch.

Acknowledgement

With gratitude to Marge Simon, Bruce Boston, and Joe & Bobbi Morey for their help in putting together this collection.

Publication History: Books, Chapbooks, & Magazines

Books:
2001-2008
A Box Full Of Alien Skies, 2001.
Bone Sprockets, 2004.
25 Cent Rocket Ship To The Stars, 2007.

2009-2013

Mortician's Tea, 2009.
Shroud Of Night, 2011.
Scenes Along The Zombie Highway, 2013.

2014-2018

Gravediggers' Dance, 2014.
The Comfort Of Screams, 2018.

Magazines:
"Leisureville", HWA Poetry Showcase, Vol. VII, 2020.
"Weeds", Not One Of Us, Issue #67, 2021.
"Oblivian's Realm", ParAbnormal, June 2021
"Tiny Houses Of The Forgotten", The Horror Zine, April 2022.
"Selfies", Star*Line, Vol. 41:3, 2020.

New Poems Original To This Collection:
Caged Fear, Faces Of Stone, A Darker Shade Of Normal, A Very Limited Engagement, Hoping For A Menu Change, A Hole In The Dark, Of Wood Chippers & Band Saws, A Smell Of Coffee And Sulfer, Leaving The Past Behind, Dead Men Walking, Ghosts Of Christmas Past, The Arms Of Death, Demon Weather, The Darkness Behind The Dark, Crime of Passion.

About the Author

Photo by Ian Clark

G. O. Clark's, (b. 1945) writing has been published in *Asimov's, Analog, Space & Time, Midnight Under The Big Top, Daily SF, HWA Poetry Showcase VII, Speculatief (BE)* and many other publications over the last 30 plus years. He's the author of 15 poetry collections, the most recent, "Easy Travel To The Stars", 2020. His 3rd fiction collection, "Aliens & Others", came out in 2021. He won the Asimov's Readers Award for poetry in 2001, and was Stoker Award Poetry finalist in 2011. He's retired, and lives in Davis, CA. surrounded by books, soothed by music, and enjoying bike ride excursions around town. http://goclarkpoet.weebly.com

www.ingramcontent.com/pod-product-compliance
Lightning Source LLC
Chambersburg PA
CBHW032359040426
42451CB00006B/66